Slavic Specialties

Collected by Dana Lumby

Front cover and section illustrations by Marjorie Kop
Design by Dana Lumby

Editors: Miriam Canter, Dorothy Crum,
Georgia Heald, and Joan Liffring-Zug Bourret

Acknowledgments

Dana Lumby, collector of the recipes and designer for *Slavic Specialties,* is a graduate of Iowa State University with a degree in Fine Arts. As an artist, writer, and graphic designer, she has designed a number of books for Penfield Press.

Marjorie Nejdl, of Cedar Rapids, Iowa, is a distinguished folk artist. Especially renowned for her Czech drawings and egg decorations, she designed the cover, section page artwork, and the egg drawings throughout the book.

Other illustrations are reproduced from paintings and prints found in historic publications.

We thank the many individuals, organizations, and official institutions who contributed recipes. Individual contributors are named with selected recipes. Organizations, who generously shared their collections are notably: *The Slovenian Women's Union of*

America, founded in 1926 by Marie Frisland. Headquartered in Joliet, Illinois, it is represented in fourteen states. Divided into seven regions, sixty-five local organizations, or "branches," meet annually. National conventions are held every four years. A cohesive force is the Union's publication ZARJA (The Dawn). Published eight months of the year, current bilingual editor Connie Leskovar of Chicago coordinates the unifying communication and sharing from each branch reporter. Irene Odorizzi, Heritage Director, Reston, Virginia, edits articles about immigrant experiences and promotes the heritage program. The traditional recipes selected for this book are from the popular cookbook, *Pots and Pans,* sponsored by the Union and compiled by Hermine Dicke, former editor of the food column in ZARJA.

The American Mutual Life Association, a fraternal organization headquartered in Cleveland, Ohio, is devoted to keeping Slovenian culture alive in the United States.

Cecilia Gaughan, Whitehall, Pennsylvania, a representative of the *Ladies' Pennsylvania Slovak Catholic Union,* contributed, along with recipes, resourceful information about traditional foods.

Thank you, also, to the Czech Embassy, the Embassy of the Republic of Bulgaria, and the Embassy of Poland, headquartered in Washington, D.C., for recipes and helpful information.

Slavic Specialties is the result of Slavic peoples from all over the United States sharing their own colorful heritage. Included are recipes from Polish, Slovak, Croatian, Slovenian, Bohemian, Russian, Bulgarian, Serbian, Czech, Bosnian, and Ukrainian Americans. These 160 pages provide only a glimpse of the complex heritage interwoven with history, language, and social orientation. Different regions have different traditions, beliefs, dress, dialect, landscape, and lifestyles, therefore, recipes vary from region to region. Some of the recipes from historic sources have been adapted to the American kitchen.

Table of Contents

A FEW COOKING TERMS…

CAPER: Pickled flower bud of the caper, used as condiment.

CRACKLINGS: The crisp bits that remain after rendering fat from meat or after frying or roasting the skin.

FARCE: A seasoned stuffing.

FARINA: Fine meal prepared from cereal grain and various other plant products and often used as a cooked cereal or in puddings.

GREENGAGE: A variety of plum, having a yellowish-green skin and sweet flesh.

ROUX: A mixture of flour and fat cooked together and used as a thickening.

SEMOLINA: Gritty, coarse particles of wheat leftover after the finer flour has passed through the bolting machine, used for pasta.

*"Identification with an ethnic group
is a source of values, instincts, ideas,
perceptions, that throw original light
on the meaning of America."*

— Michael Novak
American philosopher and theologian
of Slovak descent

Beverages

Drawing by Marjorie Kopecek Nejdl.

Dandelion Wine

Recipe from Cherished Czech Recipes

1 gallon dandelion blossoms
1 gallon water
2 lemons, sliced

2 oranges, sliced
5 cups sugar
1/2 cake yeast (per gallon of water)

Boil dandelion blossoms in water until liquor is fragrant. Strain. Add lemons and oranges to strained hot liquid. Add sugar and set aside to cool. When mixture is cold, add 1/2 cake yeast, crumbled, to each gallon of liquid. Let stand for 1 week. Remove lemons and oranges on the second or third day. After another week, pour wine into open jugs. Put loose cover, such as towel or paper, over jugs. Allow the air to circulate. Cork jugs after 2 or 3 days.

Spiced Wine

Recipe from Cherished Czech Recipes

2 (25.6-oz.) bottles red wine
1/2 lb. sugar
1 lemon peel, grated

1 stick cinnamon (small)
whole cloves (several)

Pour wine into kettle, preferably porcelain; add half pound of sugar, grated lemon peel, cinnamon and several cloves. Place on low heat long enough for flavors to mix. Do not boil. Strain before storing or serving.

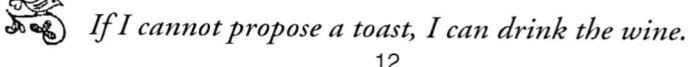 *If I cannot propose a toast, I can drink the wine.*

Iced Coffee

Recipe from Pleasing Polish Recipes

1/2 cup sugar
5 cups strong coffee
1 cup vanilla ice cream, divided

1/4 cup vodka, divided
2 cups whipped cream

Combine sugar and coffee. Chill several hours. Place 1/4 cup ice cream in each of 4 serving glasses. Add 1/2 ounce (1 tablespoon) vodka to each glass. Divide the coffee mixture among the glasses and serve topped with whipped cream.

 A wise man walks slow
but reaches his goal quickly.

Mead

Recipe from Polish Touches, Recipes and Traditions

1 quart strained honey
3 quarts water
nutmeg
pieces of ginger

piece of dried orange peel
1 tsp. hops
1 tsp. juniper berries
3 Tbsp. fresh yeast

Cook honey with the water for 1 hour. Place nutmeg, ginger, orange peel, hops, and juniper berries in a piece of cheesecloth, tie it closed, secure a weight on the end and place in honey mixture. Boil another hour. Remove spice bouquet. Cool honey mixture and place in a carboy, an airtight container that will allow gases

(Continued)

(Mead continued)

to escape but will not allow air to enter. (Carboys can be found at wine- and beer-making shops.) Dissolve the yeast in a little of the honey mixture, then add to the mead. Seal carboy. Mead will ferment at room temperature for 6 months. When the mead is fermented it will stop bubbling. Place carboy in a cool dry place. After a year, the mead should be through fermenting. Transfer it to bottles and seal the tops. Watch for delayed fermentation and if observed, open the bottle to allow the fermentation to finish, then close again. If fermentation occurs in a sealed bottle, the container will most likely explode. The longer the mead ages the better it gets.

 The morning is wiser than the evening.

Juniper Vodka

Recipe from Pleasing Polish Recipes

1/2 cup juniper berries, crushed
1 quart grain alcohol

2 cups water, divided
1 lb. sugar

Soak crushed juniper berries in the alcohol and 1 cup of water for a week. Boil sugar and remaining water until syrupy. Strain juniper alcohol through blotting paper or other filter. Add to the sugar mixture. Cool. Seal in a carboy or other container that will allow gases to escape. After a few months, when fermentation ceases, bottle and seal. The outcome is similar to gin but stronger.

"He who is satisfied with little is not so poor as he who never has enough."

Cranberry Kissel

Russian dessert drink

Serve hot or cold with cream. Use raspberries, red currants, black currants, or blackberries, but the sugar must be added in proportion to the sweetness of the berries.

4 cups cranberries
2 cups water
2 cups sugar

1/2 tsp. cinnamon
2 Tbsp. cornstarch
whipped cream, for topping

Put the cranberries into a saucepan with the water. Boil until berries pop (about 10 minutes). Crush the cranberries thoroughly, and strain them. Place the cranberry purée in a saucepan and add the sugar, cinnamon, cornstarch, and a

(Continued)

(Cranberry Kissel continued)

little water—mixing well the whole time. Bring the mixture to a boil, stirring constantly, and cook for 5 minutes. Place in the refrigerator to cool. Serve in individual glasses, with whipped cream. *(Serves 8)*

Detail of embroidery sample from *Podunajská Dedina v Ceskoslovensku.*

Soups & Stews

Drawing by Marjorie Kopecek Nejdl.

Beef Stew

Recipe of Katie Papich, mother of Penfield Press editor Dorothy Papich Crum.

Croatian beef stew with bell peppers (paprikash).

1 lb. stewing beef, cut into small chunks
1 large onion, chopped
2 cloves garlic, minced
3 carrots, pared and cut into 1/2-inch pieces
3 medium-size bell peppers, seeded, cut into 1/2-inch pieces

6 medium-size fresh tomatoes, skinned, or 1 28-oz. can whole tomatoes
2 whole cloves
1 bay leaf
1 tsp. paprika
salt and pepper, to taste

(Continued)

(Beef Stew continued)

In a large skillet or Dutch oven, brown the beef. Add onion and cook over moderate heat until onion is tender. Add the garlic, carrots, and peppers. Sauté lightly for a few minutes, then add tomatoes, cloves, bay leaf, paprika, and salt and pepper to taste. Cover and cook at low to moderate temperature for about 2 hours. Stir occasionally. *(Serves 8)*

Tip: Serve with *Polenta* recipe on page 48.

 Who has the shore, has the sea, and the castle is his who holds the plain, but freedom dwells on the peaks of the mountain.

Slovenian Barley Soup

Slovenian recipe contributed by Alice Kuhar, Cleveland, Ohio

A favorite with the children and family on cold winter days.

1 1/2 cups medium pearl barley
1 1/2 to 2 lbs. smoked meat
 (either cottage ham, smoked
 pork chops, pork loin, smoked
 sausage, or ham bone with meat)
1 medium-size carrot, sliced

1 medium-size potato, diced
1 fresh tomato, quartered
1 Tbsp. salt
few sprigs of parsley
1 clove garlic
1 medium-size onion

Wash barley thoroughly and drain. Place in a large soup pot. Add meat, carrots, potatoes, tomato, and salt. Cut a square of cheesecloth or clean white cloth and

(Continued)

(Slovenian Barley Soup continued)

place parsley, garlic and onion in center of it. Gather edges together and tie securely with a string. Drop this bouquet garnish into soup pot and add 2 quarts water, adding more if soup becomes too thick while cooking. Bring to a boil, lower heat, and simmer for 1 1/2 to 2 hours. Soup will be thick. *(Serves 6-8)*

Note: This is a thick hearty soup and is excellent served with a thick slice of crusty homemade bread.

 It is better to weep with the wise than to sing with fools; it is better to fight with a hero than to kiss a coward.

Beer Soup with Egg Yolks

Polish recipe contributed by the Embassy of the Republic of Poland, Washington, D.C.

1 1/3 pints light beer
3/4 pint water
2–3 cloves garlic
dash of cinnamon

4 egg yolks, beaten
1/2 cup sugar
croutons
1 Tbsp. butter

In a large pot, bring to a boil the light beer with the water, garlic, and cinnamon. Lower the heat and slowly add the egg yolks with the sugar, stirring constantly, until thoroughly heated. Do not boil. Serve topped with croutons fried in butter. *(Serves 4)*

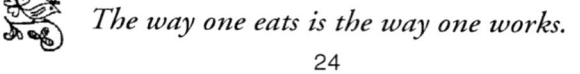

The way one eats is the way one works.

Beef Soup (Goveja juha)

Slovenian recipe by Albina Novak, Chicago, Illinois, contributed by the Slovenian Women's Union of America.

1 1/2 lbs. beef and
  some extra bones
1 small slice of liver
  (pork or beef)
4 quarts water
1 whole onion, halved
2 stalks celery with tops
1 clove garlic or dash of
  garlic salt

1 small slice yellow turnip
1 small cabbage wedge
2 tomatoes or 2/3 cup purée or
  tomato paste
2 medium-size carrots, scraped
1 small parsnip, peeled
2 sprigs parsley
1 Tbsp. salt
1/4 tsp. pepper or 5 peppercorns

(Continued)

(Beef Soup continued)

Place all ingredients in a large pot and bring to boil. Reduce heat and simmer 2 hours. Strain to another pot. To the clear, boiling broth, add noodles, farina or liver dumplings (see pp. 71), rice or whatever your family enjoys. **Tip:** The boiled meat may be added, along with sliced carrots, celery and onion pieces.

Drawings by Marjorie Kopecek Nejdl.

Beef Browned Soup (Prežgana juha)

Slovenian recipe by Jean Jelenc, Milwaukee, Wisconsin. Recipe tip by Mary Bostian, Euclid, Ohio. Contributed by the Slovenian Women's Union of America.

This is a traditional recipe brought to America by Slovenian immigrants. Homemade lard was used instead of butter.

2 Tbsp. butter or oleo
2 Tbsp. flour
1/2 tsp. salt, or to taste

3 cups boiling beef broth or bouillon
croutons (from toasted bread), optional

Egg Noodles:
2 eggs
1 tsp. white vinegar (optional)

1/2 tsp. caraway seed (optional)

(Continued)

Soup: Melt butter or oleo over medium heat in skillet. Blend in flour and salt and cook, stirring, until brown. Slowly add the broth or bouillon and bring to a boil. Pour in beaten eggs to form egg noodles (recipe follows). Simmer for 3 minutes. If desired, serve the soup garnished with croutons made from toasted bread.

Egg Noodles: Heat broth to a rapid boil. Meanwhile, beat eggs with a fork in a cup until egg runs off in a watery stream. Pour eggs in a fine stream from cup held about 5 inches above saucepan while stirring soup with a fork. The egg, as it cooks, forms noodle-like shreds. Simmer for 3 minutes. *(Serves 2)*

Tip: For additional flavor add white vinegar and/or caraway seed to the eggs.

Thin Porridge (Močnik)

Slovenian recipe by Christina Zupancic, Duluth, Minnesota. Recipe tip by Katie Tuzak, Chicago, Illinois. Contributed by the Slovenian Women's Union of America.

An old Slovenian recipe.

2 quarts (8 cups) boiling salted
  water or chicken or beef broth
1 3/4 cups flour
2 eggs
1 1/2 tsp. salt

pinch of crushed mint
  (*milesa*), if desired
2 Tbsp. butter
1/4 cup breadcrumbs
snipped parsley

Bring salted water (add bouillon cubes, if desired) or broth to boil. Meanwhile in bowl, mix flour and eggs with a fork, and then work with fingers to form fine

(Continued)

crumbles—using up all the flour. Very slowly (or a mass will form) add crumbles to the boiling liquid, stirring constantly with a fork. Simmer for 15 minutes, stirring occasionally, until consistency of thin oatmeal. Add salt and pinch of crushed mint if desired. Melt butter and add breadcrumbs to brown. Pour *Močnik* into soup bowls and garnish with the browned breadcrumbs and snipped parsley.

Tip: "My mother used milk instead of water or broth and served it for breakfast. When using milk, she added 1 tablespoon butter and 1 teaspoon sugar."

 If you have had enough of your friend, grant him a loan.

Beet Soup (Borsch)

Russian recipe

2 1/2 lbs. rich soup meat,
   cut into bite-size pieces
3–4 quarts water
2 onions, peeled, very finely
   chopped
1/4 lb. butter, for frying
1 1/4 lbs. beets, peeled, and
   cut into long, thin strips
2 turnips, finely cut
2 carrots, finely cut

5/8 lb. fresh cabbage, chopped
   very fine (as for coleslaw)
2 Tbsp. flour
1/2 lb. ham bone, cooked
vinegar, salt, pepper, bay leaves,
   allspice, to taste
5–8 tomatoes, finely sliced
5 Tbsp. sour cream
cooked duck or chicken pieces,
   sliced thin (optional)

(Continued)

Cut the meat, add water, and boil to make regular white bouillon. While this is cooking, prepare separately the following: chop the onions, and fry in butter in a deep saucepan. Add the beets. Let the beets and onions cook for some time, uncovered. Add turnips, carrots and 2 tablespoons of soup stock. When these vegetables are quite cooked, add the cabbage. When this is slightly cooked, add the flour and cook a little more. About 1–1 1/2 hours before serving, when all the vegetables are fully-cooked, add the bouillon, pouring it through a very fine strainer. Wash off the cooked meat and add to the soup, letting all boil over low heat, uncovered. Add the cooked ham bone, vinegar, salt, pepper, a few grains allspice, and bay leaves. Thirty minutes before serving, add the tomatoes. Just before serving, skim extra fat off the soup and add sour cream *(Serves 10-12 generously)*

(Continued)

(Beet Soup continued)

Tip: To vary the flavor: just before serving, add any cold, cooked fowl, such as duck or chicken.

Mushroom Sauerkraut Soup

From the menu of a Slovak supper contributed by Cecilia Gaughan, Whitehall, Pennsylvania, of the Ladies Pennsylvania Slovak Catholic Union.

The supper begins with a prayer and toast offered by the head of the family. We then have oplatky *(wafers) to begin our meal. Next, we each take an English walnut for good luck and good health. We cut up an apple into as many slices as we have people at the table and share the apple for unity. Then, we have our very special soup. Each part of Slovakia has its own. My parents came from the central part of Slovakia, near Bratislava.*

2 lbs. large, dry lima beans
2 1/4 lbs. fresh, white mushrooms,
   cleaned

2 large cans sauerkraut
   (Silver Floss brand—preferable)

(Continued)

Brown sauce:

1/2 lb. butter

1 1/2 cups flour

Reserved mushroom and
sauerkraut liquids

Soak the beans overnight. The next morning, drain and cover with 8 cups of unsalted water. Cook for at least 2 hours, and then salt to taste. Cook for about 15 minutes more, until the beans are soft. Do not drain. Place the mushrooms in another pan, cover with water, and bring to a boil. Cook for 30 minutes. Rinse sauerkraut twice in cold water. Cover with water, and bring to a boil, cooking for about 30 minutes. Remove the mushrooms and sauerkraut from the heat. Strain the mushrooms and sauerkraut and reserve the juice in separate containers. Add

(Continued)

the mushrooms and sauerkraut to beans. Add equal measurements of reserved mushroom and sauerkraut juice to make the consistency of soup. Let this stand, on very low heat, until you make your brown sauce.

Directions for brown sauce: Mix together, over low heat, the butter and flour, until light brown. Start adding by spoonfuls into the soup, stirring constantly. If the soup becomes too thick, add remaining juice from mushrooms and sauerkraut. Cook over low heat for about 45 minutes, stirring often. *(Makes about 10 quarts. Sufficient for a large family and friends.)*

TIP: This soup is much better after it stands. Prepare the day before if possible, and reheat on Christmas Eve. Freezes well.

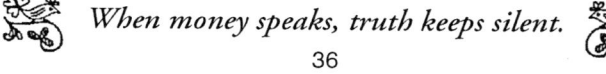 *When money speaks, truth keeps silent.*

White Bean Soup

Yugoslavian

1 1/2 cups dried white beans
1/2 cup olive or vegetable oil
2 medium-size onions, peeled
  and chopped
1 stalk of celery, chopped
2 garlic cloves, crushed

1 large carrot, scraped and minced
2 tomatoes, peeled and chopped
1/2 tsp. crumbled dried thyme
1 bay leaf (optional)
salt and pepper, to taste

Soak beans overnight or for several hours. Drain and add 8 cups water. Bring to a boil. Lower heat; cook slowly, covered. Meanwhile, heat oil in a skillet. Add onions and celery. Sauté until limp. Add garlic, carrot and tomatoes. Sauté 5

(Continued)

minutes; stir into beans. Add thyme and bay leaf (if desired). Season with salt and pepper. Continue to cook until beans and carrots are tender—about 1 1/2 hours. (*Serves 6-8*)

Tip: Very good served with cornbread.

Squash-Vegetable Stew

Bosnian

1 medium-size eggplant,
  washed
1 yellow squash, washed
1 cup olive oil
1 medium-size onion, peeled
  and chopped

2 medium-size tomatoes, peeled
  and chopped
2 garlic cloves, crushed
1/4 cup chopped fresh parsley
1/2 tsp. dried marjoram
salt and pepper, to taste

Remove stems from eggplants and squash and cut into cubes. Heat oil in a saucepan; sauté onions in oil until tender. Add eggplant and squash cubes; sauté 1 or 2 minutes. Stir in other ingredients. Cook slowly, covered, for about 25 minutes, or until eggplant and squash are cooked. Stir occasionally. *(Serves 4-6)*

Breads

Drawing by Marjorie Kopecek Nejdl.

Walnut Roll (Orehova Potica)

Slovenian recipe by Jean Krizman, Cleveland, Ohio, contributed by the Slovenian Women's Union of America.

Foremost in Slovenian cuisine is Potica. *It is primarily Slovenian with the name derived from the word* povitica *which means "something rolled in." At social gatherings or festive occasions,* Potica *is served, unbuttered, either as bread with the main part of the meal or as dessert with coffee. It is as Slovenian as Apple Pie is American. The following detailed recipe is for the very beginner.* Walnut Potica *is really a nut roll made in three parts: a yeast dough, a rich walnut filling and the rolling process. Among the Slovenians, it is a real delicacy at holiday time to make ham sandwiches with* potica *and grated fresh horseradish.*

(Continued)

Yeast dough:

2 cakes (5/8 oz. each) compressed
  yeast or 3 pkgs. dry yeast
1/2 cup warm milk
1 Tbsp. sugar
4 egg yolks, well beaten
1/4 lb. butter (1 stick)
1 cup milk, heated

1 cup sour cream
1 tsp. salt
1/3 cup sugar
1 tsp. vanilla
1 tsp. grated lemon rind
6–7 1/2 cups all-purpose flour

Rolling process ingredients:

1 unbeaten egg white

1 whole egg plus 1 Tbsp. water

(Continued)

Rich walnut filling:

1 cup honey
1 cup milk
1 cup cream (sweet or sour)
1/4 lb. butter (1 stick)
1 1/2 cups sugar

1 1/2 lbs. walnuts, finely ground
 to fill 6 cups
1 Tbsp. grated lemon rind
1 Tbsp. vanilla or rum flavoring
4 egg whites, stiffly beaten

Yeast dough directions: Dissolve yeast in warm milk and 1 tablespoon of sugar. Let stand until foamy. Add beaten egg yolks and set aside. Melt butter in heated milk; blend in sour cream, salt and 1/3 cup sugar. Cool. Stir in vanilla and lemon rind. Combine with egg-yeast mixture. In a large bowl, place 6 cups flour; reserve

(Continued)

the remaining 1 1/2 cups. Make a well in flour; pour in combined liquid mixture. With a wooden spoon, mix until all liquid is absorbed, adding only enough reserved flour to handle dough more easily. Place on floured board and knead 15–20 minutes until dough is smooth and elastic. Add small amounts of flour, if necessary, until dough is no longer sticky. (Kneading can also be done with an electric mixer and a dough hook.) Place dough in a greased bowl. Turn dough upside down to grease top. Cover with a cloth and let rise until double, about 1 1/2 to 2 hours.

Walnut Filling directions: Heat honey, milk, cream, butter and sugar until butter melts. Do not boil. In food chopper, with finest blade, grind walnuts. Pour hot mixture over ground walnuts. Stir and cool. Add grated lemon rind and flavoring. Fold in beaten egg whites and set aside.

44

(Continued)

Rolling process: Grease well three 12x4-inch pans or four 9x5-inch bread loaf pans. Place fully-raised dough on a lengthy floured cloth on a table which is large enough to roll dough to 30x40 inches. (To make rolling easier, a flannel cloth, or old clean mattress cover might be used under the floured cloth as a padding.) Roll out all the dough. To give uniformity to the center of the rolled *potica*, trim about 1/2 inch of dough along wider edge, closest to you. (This can be formed into small rolls and baked separately—they are referred to as "končke" in Slovenian.) With spatula, spread filling on dough evenly, covering entire surface except 3 inches at wider end of dough, to be rolled up last. Start rolling dough with fingers, tightly at first, along trimmed edge; stretch dough slightly as you continue to roll, to tighten, and keep side edges as even as possible.

(Continued)

When half rolled, prick roll with a thin knitting needle or a skewer, about every 2 inches, halfway through. This prevents *potica* from cracking while it bakes. Continue to roll until 3 inches from end. Paint this unfilled area with egg white, which will give a seal at the seam of the roll.

Panning: When shaped into a long roll, prick again and line up your pans (three 12x4 inches or four 9x5 inches). Use the edge of a flat plate to cut through the roll in lengths to fit pans. Push dough together to seal in the filling. Fit into greased pans.

Proofing and baking: Cover and let rise 1/2 to 1 hour until doubled. Beat 1 egg with 1 tablespoon water and brush over loaves. Bake in 325° oven for 1 hour. Remove from oven and let cool in pans for 15 minutes. Remove from pan, place on a wire rack and let cool completely.

(Continued)

(Walnut Roll continued)

Tips: To prevent drying, wrap *potica* in foil or waxed paper, or place in plastic bags and store in refrigerator (about 2 weeks). Freeze up to 6 months.

Drawings by
Marjorie Kopecek Nejdl.

Apple Roll

Czech recipe from The Congressional Club Cookbook, ©1927

2 cups flour
1 egg yolk
salt

3 Tbsp. butter, melted
lukewarm water
powdered sugar

Filling:

apples, pared and sliced thin
butter, melted
breadcrumbs
sugar

cinnamon
almonds, chopped
Sultana raisins
   (small, yellow, seedless)

(Apple Roll continued)

Work together flour, egg yolk, salt and butter. Add enough water to make a soft dough. Knead well and set aside, covered with a plate, for 1 hour. In the meantime, prepare the filling ingredients.

Filling: Spread a clean cloth on the table and flour it. Turn out the dough in the center. Roll out slightly and brush over with melted butter. With lightly floured hands, stretch the dough until it becomes thin and transparent. Sprinkle with melted butter, breadcrumbs, almonds, apples, raisins, sugar, and cinnamon. Butter again; roll up; brush over with butter and put in buttered pan. Bake in a moderate oven (350°) for about 30 minutes. Cut into slices. Sprinkle with powdered sugar before serving.

 Music and song are the natural gift of the whole Slav race.

Czech Kolache

Czech recipe from The Congressional Club Cookbok ©1927

1 cup of lukewarm milk
1/4 lb. butter, melted
2 egg yolks
1 egg white
2 cups flour
1 cake of yeast, dissolved in
   1/4 cup of lukewarm water

1/3 cup sugar
pinch of salt
grated lemon rind
1 egg, beaten
marmalade or other filling
1/2 cup melted butter
powdered sugar

Dissolve yeast in 1/4 cup warm milk. Beat together milk, butter, 2 egg yolks, 1 egg white, and flour. Add yeast, sugar, salt, and lemon rind. Work it well (the

(Continued)

dough should not be stiff). Put aside to rise. Toss on floured board, cut into small pieces, shape into small balls and place on buttered baking pan 4 inches apart. Press each ball flat and indent center with thumb or spoon. Brush edges with beaten egg. Fill center with marmalade or other filling. Let rise again and bake in moderate oven (350°). When done, brush over with melted butter and sprinkle with powdered sugar.

Popular fillings: butter rum; cabbage; cherry; honey-poppy seed; nut butter; prune; berries; to name a few.

> *"Go to villages, cross the meadows, pass the pastures, and commons everywhere, yes, everywhere songs will greet you! And what songs!"*
> —*Anonymous comment about Bohemia*—

Pancakes (Blini)

Russian recipe from The Congressional Club Cookbook, ©1927

1 oz. yeast, compressed or dry
1 quart milk, lukewarm
5 cups flour, divided

5 eggs, separated
6 Tbsp. butter, softened
salt and pepper, to taste

Dissolve the yeast in warm milk and pour into deep pan. Add one-half of the portion of flour. When well mixed, allow to sit in warm place for 1–1 1/2 hours. Beat the egg yolks and the butter thoroughly and add with the remaining flour and salt to yeast mixture when it has risen well. Mix and let rise for another 30–45 minutes. To the raised dough, add beaten egg whites and taking only a

(Continued)

spoonful of batter at a time, fry in small pans with a little butter. Spread with butter before turning over to brown on the other side. The *blini* should be very thin, almost as thin as sheets of paper.

Tip: Sour cream, butter, finely-sliced smoked salmon, and fresh beluga caviar may be served with *blini*.

Dumplings & Cereals

Drawing by Marjorie Kopecek Nejdl.

Cornmeal Mush (Polenta)

Slovenian recipe by Anne Kompare, Chicago, Illinois, contributed by the Slovenian Women's Union of America.

2 cups boiling water

1 1/2 cups cornmeal (yellow)

2 cups cold water

1 tsp. salt

In upper pan of double boiler over direct heat, heat 2 cups water to boiling. In bowl, mix cornmeal with cold water and salt. Slowly pour the cornmeal mixture into boiling water and cook over direct heat, stirring, until mixture thickens and cooks (2 minutes). Place over lower pan with boiling water to steam covered for 30 minutes, stirring occasionally.

To serve: *Polenta* is frequently served hot on a platter in large spoonfuls to be

(Continued)

(Cornmeal Mush continued)

topped with beef goulash or smothered with beef or pork gravy. It is an excellent side dish for pork or beef roast dinners. It may be served with melted butter and sour cream, or the next day, sliced and fried in butter, topped with maple syrup. *(Serves 8)*

Potato Dumplings

Czech appetizer contributed by the Embassy of the Czech Republic, Washington, D.C.

5–6 large baking potatoes, unpeeled
2 eggs
2 cups flour (preferably Wondra)

1/2 cup Cream of Wheat
2 Tbsp. cornstarch
1 tsp. salt

Cook the potatoes, unpeeled, in a good-size pot. Set aside to cool, then peel and mash. Combine the eggs, flour, Cream of Wheat, cornstarch, and salt into a firm dough. Shape the dough into rolls, 2 inches in diameter, and place these in a large pot of boiling water. Boil for about 20 minutes, then lift one by one, carefully, and cut each into slices. *(Serves 6-8)*

 Woe to the legs under a foolish head.

Stuffed Dumplings (Pyzy)

Polish recipe contributed by Richard Vitkay of Albany, New York

"These are more work than pierogi, *but definitely worth it. I have seen them only in one Polish restaurant, a small one in New Jersey, run by an immigrant Pole."*

Pyzy:

1 lb. potatoes, divided
1/4 cup flour

1/2 tsp. salt
1/2 tsp. pepper

Filling:

1/2 cup cooked meat, minced or ground. (Meat may be of your choice.)

1/2 small onion, finely chopped or grated
3 Tbsp. gravy

58

(Continued)

Topping:

1/2 cup bacon, cooked, diced   butter

Boil 1/2 lb. potatoes in skins until tender (about 20 minutes). Drain, cool and peel. Put through a sieve. Peel and grate the remaining 1/2 lb. potatoes; squeeze to remove liquid. Mix the cooked and uncooked potato with flour, salt, and pepper. Beat the mixture until it becomes soft dough. You may have to add more flour. In a separate bowl, combine the filling ingredients. Divide the soft dough into 8 parts. Flour your hands. Take a portion of potato dough and flatten into a patty. Place 1/8th of the filling on the patty. Mold the patty around it to make a ball. Shape the rest of the dumplings. Bring a pot of water to a simmer. Cook

(Continued)

(Stuffed Dumplings continued)

the dumplings for 5–7 minutes. The *pyzy* will rise to the surface when fully cooked. They should look slightly glossy and feel firm. While the dumplings are cooking, brown the bacon and dice. Transfer the *pyzy* to a warmed serving dish and top with bacon and melted butter. *(Serves 4)*

*Drawings by
Marjorie Kopecek Nejdl.*

Dough Pockets (Pierogi)

Polish recipes by Maria Lemnis and Henryk Vitry.
Contributed by the Embassy of the Republic of Poland, Washington, D.C.

Pierogi, *a popular dish most likely originating from the older Slavic folk cuisine, is inexpensive, nourishing and very tasty. The following seven pages include a recipe for the dough, and five variations for the filling.*

Dough:

1 3/4–2 cups flour
pinch of salt
1 large egg

1/2–3/4 cup water
butter or pork fat (with cracklings)
thick, lightly soured cream

(Continued)

Dough: Put flour, mixed with salt on a pastry board. Make a well, drop in the egg and knead to form a dough. Add a little lukewarm water in order to get a quite loose dough which is very well-kneaded and does not stick to the hands or pastry board. Divide the dough into 4 parts. Cover the remaining dough with a bowl or towel so it does not dry. Then roll each part out thinly. With a teacup or wineglass, cut out circles that are 2–2 1/2 inches in diameter. Place a heaping teaspoonful of the filling on each circle. Fold over and press the edges firmly so that it does not open during cooking. The shaping of *pierogi* itself calls for a little experience, as they should be neat, not crushed, well-filled, and well-sealed at the edges. Cook the shaped *pierogi* in a shallow wide pot, in a large amount of lightly salted water. When they come to the surface, cook them over low heat for 4–5

(Continued)

minutes more, then remove with a large strainer spoon and drain well. Place them on a dish. Pour butter or pork fat (with cracklings) over the *pierogi*. Serve with thick, lightly soured cream. They may be served directly after cooking, or fried when cool. These are the standard steps in the preparation of *pierogi*. (Makes 12 to 18)

The following *Pierogi* fillings are traditional, but you can vary according to taste.

Russian *Pierogi*:

1 lb. cooked potatoes, peeled
3/4 cup cottage cheese
1 medium-size onion,
    finely chopped

1 egg
salt and pepper, to taste

63

(Continued)

(Dough Pockets continued)

Put the cooked potatoes and cottage cheese through a meat grinder. Sauté the onions to a golden brown. Add to the potato mixture; stir in the egg. Season to taste with salt and pepper. Fill the *pierogi* and cook accordingly.

Sweet Cabbage *Pierogi*: Pierogi *made with a farce (seasoned stuffing) of sweet cabbage or sauerkraut are very popular.*

1 2-lb. head of sweet cabbage,
  cooked
salt water for simmering
1 medium-size onion,
  finely chopped

butter or lard
salt and pepper, to taste
a few mushrooms, cooked, drained
1 hard-cooked egg, finely chopped
  (optional)

(Continued)

(Dough Pockets continued)

Cook the cabbage in salted water. Remove, and chop finely. Sauté the onion in butter or lard. Add the cabbage to the browned onions and simmer until tender. Add salt and pepper to taste. Add mushrooms to the stock, and cook until the mixture is thick enough. Add the egg (optional). Fill *pierogi* and cook accordingly.

Sauerkraut *Pierogi:*

2 lbs. sauerkraut
4 Tbsp. fat (pork or butter)
1 medium-size onion, fried

salt and pepper, to taste
breadcrumbs
mushrooms, cooked,
    finely chopped

65

(Continued)

Simmer the sauerkraut in the fat, adding a fried onion, salt and pepper, some breadcrumbs, and mushrooms. Fill *pierogi* and cook accordingly.

Pierogi with Cheese:

1 lb. cottage cheese, well-drained   salt, to taste
1 small egg

Rub the cottage cheese through a wire sieve, then mix thoroughly with the egg and moderate amount of salt. This filling swells during cooking, so do not use too much. Fill *pierogi* and cook accordingly. Serve immediately after cooking. Do not reheat these.

(Continued)

Sweet *Pierogi* with Cheese: *These are a very nourishing dessert.*

Dough:

2 cups flour
3 Tbsp. butter
1 egg

1 egg yolk
1/2 cup lukewarm water
pinch of salt

Filling:

1 lb. creamed cottage cheese
4–6 Tbsp. sugar

1 Tbsp. candied orange peel, very
    finely diced
4 Tbsp. small raisins

Combine dough ingredients, knead, and shape *pierogi*.

Filling: Put the cottage cheese through a sieve. Mix creamed cottage cheese with

67

(Continued)

sugar. Add the orange peel and raisins. Fill *pierogi* and cook accordingly. Do not reheat these.

Dumplings-Potato (Kopytka)

Polish recipes by Maria Lemnis and Henryk Vitry.
Contributed by the Embassy of the Republic of Poland, Washington, D.C.

2 lbs. potatoes, peeled, cooked
1 large egg
1 3/4–2 cups flour
salt, to taste

hot butter or pork fat, with
 cracklings
1 small onion, finely chopped
 (optional)

Rub cooked, warm potatoes through a sieve, or put through a meat grinder. Cool the potatoes and beat in the egg. Add the flour and salt, and mix. Place on a pastry board dusted with flour, and knead to a smooth dough. Divide the dough into 3–4 parts. Form into finger-thick rolls and slice diagonally into small 1-inch-

(Continued)

long dumplings. Cook in a large amount of salted boiling water. Take out the cooked *kopytka* with a straining spoon and drain well. Place dumplings on a dish. Pour hot butter or pork fat with cracklings over them. A chopped onion may be fried in the pork fat.

Tip: The *kopytka*, except the topping, may be cooked a day ahead. Before serving, drop them into boiling salted water, bring to a boil and remove. They also taste great if reheated by frying.

> *If one should imbed a Slavic desire beneath a fortress*
> *it would raise it from the ground.*
> —*Joseph de Maistre*—

Farina Dumplings

*Recipe by Albina Novak, Chicago, Illinois, contributed by the
Slovenian Women's Union of America.*

1 egg
1/2 tsp. salt
1 Tbsp. oil or melted butter

1/3 cup farina
1 quart beef broth

Beat egg; stir in salt, oil or melted butter and farina. Let stand for 10 minutes without stirring. Bring a clear beef soup to a boil. First dip teaspoon into boiling soup, then drop rounded teaspoonfuls of mixture into boiling soup. Reduce heat and simmer, covered for 15 minutes. Cook at least 15 minutes for large, delicate dumplings. *(Makes about 9 dumplings)*
(Beef Soup recipe, P. 25)

Farina Štruklji (Zdrobovi štruklji)

Recipe by Milena Gobetz, Willoughby Hills, Ohio, contributed by the Slovenian Women's Union of America.

"We like it served with homemade vegetable soup and apple sauce or fruit compote."

2 tsp. salt in 4 quarts water
1/4 lb. butter, room temperature
3/4 cup sugar
1 cup regular farina or Cream of
Wheat
4 eggs

1 tsp. salt
1 carton (16 oz.) creamed cottage
cheese
6 slices bread, cubed
raisins (optional)
browned breadcrumbs

In a large kettle or roaster, bring salted water to boil. With wooden spoon, mix

(Continued)

together the butter, sugar, farina or Cream of Wheat, eggs and salt. Add cottage cheese and cubed bread (if you cut bread while it is still frozen, you can make very small cubes). If desired, stir in raisins. Let the mixture stand for a few minutes. Wet a linen towel (about 30 inches long). Spoon the mixture in a thick line, close to the edge of the towel. Leave about 2 inches from end for a 26-inch roll. Wrap roll in the towel and tie with string at one end. Make several turns with string along roll and tie opposite end. Place in boiling water and cook, covered, for 20 minutes (if you use farina, the cooking time is about 15 minutes). Keep water boiling gently. Remove from water, cut string, and unroll towel carefully. Drain and cut the *štruklji* into 1 or 2-inch slices; top with browned bread crumbs.

Vegetables

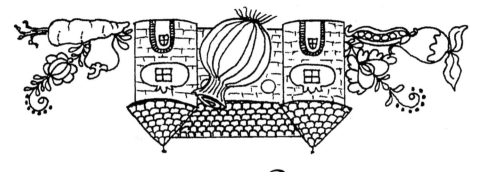

Drawing by Marjorie Kopecek Nejdl.

Mother Kalina's Zucchini with Rice

Bulgarian recipe contributed by Rumiana Ivanov of New York, New York

1 medium-size, white onion
1/2 cup vegetable oil
   (safflower or sunflower)
2–3 cloves garlic, finely chopped
1 carrot cut into thin, round slices
1 red pepper cut into small pieces

1/2 cup medium-grain rice
1/2 cup lukewarm water
3 medium-size zucchini, peeled
   and cut into 1/4"-round slices
1 tsp. finely chopped dill
salt and black pepper, to taste

Sauté onion in vegetable oil for 5 minutes. Add garlic and sauté for 5 more minutes. Add carrot and red pepper and sauté 5 minutes. Add rice, stirring the mixture constantly for 2–3 minutes. Add water and zucchini and bring to a boil.

75

(Continued)

Cover and simmer on low heat for about 20 minutes, or until rice is done. Stir only once or twice while simmering. When the rice is ready, add dill, salt and pepper (to taste), and stir. Turn off the heat. Leave covered for 1/2 hour before serving. *(Serves 4–6)*

TIP: In Bulgaria, this dish is often served with yogurt, black olives and/or green salad.

Slovak-Style Beans

Slovak recipe contributed by Richard Vitkay of Albany, New York

"My mother learned how to make these from my father's mother (her mother-in-law). It was the only way my mother could get my siblings and me to eat wax beans. It is still a favorite in all our families."

1 lb. yellow wax beans or green string beans	sour cream (enough to coat)
1 medium-size onion, chopped	salt and pepper, to taste
butter for frying	paprika

Cook the beans to desired tenderness in boiling water. Meanwhile, sauté the onion in butter until a golden color. Drain beans. Mix with cooked onions. Add

(Continued)

enough sour cream to coat the beans. Add seasonings. Transfer to a warmed serving dish. Sprinkle with paprika and serve. *(Serves 4-6)*

Leeks with Rice

Bulgarian recipe contributed by the Embassy of the Republic of Bulgaria

3–4 leeks
1/2 cup vegetable oil
1 cup rice

3 cups water
2–3 tomatoes
salt and black pepper, to taste

Cut washed leeks into 1-inch pieces and sauté in vegetable oil until tender. Add rice and water, tomatoes, salt, black pepper and simmer, covered, about 20 minutes, or until the water is almost evaporated. Turn off the heat and let sit, covered, until the water is completely absorbed. *(Serves 4-6)*

"The gift of the Slav for color and music touches the whole life with poetry."
—Emily Greene Balch—

Marrows (Squash) with Mayonnaise

Bulgarian recipe contributed by the Embassy of the Republic of Bulgaria

3–4 small marrows (squash)
  cut into large cubes
1 small bunch dill

1 1/2–2 Tbsp. mayonnaise
salt, to taste
garlic, crushed (optional)

Wash, stem, scrape, and cut marrows. Boil in salted water until soft. Strain and sprinkle generously with chopped dill. Cover with mayonnaise. Add salt, to taste, and garlic, if desired. *(Serves 2-4)*

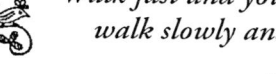

Walk fast and you catch misfortune;
walk slowly and it catches you.

Sauerkraut with Potatoes and Dumplings

Slovak recipe contributed by Dorothy Jurcenko of Chicago, Illinois

2 small potatoes
1 27-oz. can sauerkraut
5 quarts water, for boiling
1 Tbsp. salt
2 cups all-purpose flour
2 eggs

1/2 tsp. baking powder
1/2 tsp. salt
1/2 cup warm water
2 sticks butter or margarine
1 large onion, chopped
salt and pepper, to taste

Peel and dice potatoes into small cubes. Cook in salted water until potatoes are tender, but not too soft. Drain and set aside. Cook sauerkraut for 20 minutes. Drain and squeeze out excess water. Set aside. Fill a kettle with 5 quarts of water.

(Continued)

(Sauerkraut with Potatoes and Dumplings continued)

Add 1 tablespoon salt, and bring to a boil. Meanwhile, in a medium-size mixing bowl, combine flour, eggs, baking powder and salt. Add 1/2 cup warm water. Mix well. Drop 1/2 teaspoonfuls into the boiling water. Simmer over medium heat about 10 minutes. The dumplings will rise to the top of the water. Drain into a colander. Melt butter in Dutch oven. Add chopped onion and sauté until transparent. Add sauerkraut, dumplings and potatoes. Cook only until warmed thoroughly—about 10 minutes. Season to taste. Serve with sausage or roast pork. *(Serves 4-6)*

If you wish to know what a man is, place him in authority.

Stuffed Peppers

Croatian dish contributed by Dorothy Crum, Iowa City, Iowa

8 large green bell peppers
1 lb. ground beef
1 lb. ground pork
1/2 cup uncooked rice
2 cloves garlic, minced
1 egg
salt and pepper, to taste

4 carrots, pared and cut into large
    chunks
4 fresh tomatoes, skinned, or
    1 14-oz. can whole tomatoes
water to cover
1 Tbsp. flour

Wash and cut stem ends off peppers; remove seeds and membrane. In a large
bowl, mix together the ground meats, rice, minced garlic, egg, salt and pepper.

(Continued)

(Stuffed Peppers continued)

Stuff whole peppers about 2/3 full with meat mixture (allowing for expansion of rice). Place stuffed peppers in a large soup kettle. Add carrots and tomatoes and enough water to cover and another 3 or 4 cups. Salt and pepper to taste. Bring to a boil; cover, reduce heat and cook for 1 1/2 hours. Mix 1 cup of the hot broth with the flour. Stir this slowly into the simmering broth and cook for 1/2 hour longer. The peppers are served with the carrots and some of the broth. *(Serves 6-8)*

Note: A hearty bread and Black Radish Salad are good accompaniments. (Black Radish Salad found on page 94.)

 The swallow carries spring on her wings.

Cauliflower with Cheese Sauce

Croatian recipe of Katie Papich, mother of Penfield editor Dorothy Papich Crum

1 large head cauliflower

Cheese Sauce:
2 Tbsp. butter or margarine
2 Tbsp. flour
2 cups milk
salt to taste
1/2 lb. sharp Cheddar cheese

dash of lemon juice (optional)

1 small bunch fresh dill, minced (optional)
1 small bunch shallots, minced (optional)

Trim outer leaves and wash cauliflower well. Place whole head in a deep pot and cover with salted water. (A dash of lemon juice will maintain white color.) Bring

(Continued)

to a boil and cook until tender, about 15 minutes. Remove cauliflower from water; drain and arrange in serving-size pieces in a buttered baking dish.

To prepare the sauce: Melt butter or margarine in a saucepan; add flour and whisk until smooth. Add milk and salt and continue to whisk until mixture thickens. Add cheese; stir until cheese melts. Add more milk if needed to reach a thick but pouring consistency. Add the dill and/or shallots if desired. Pour the sauce over cauliflower in baking dish and reheat at 350° for about 20 minutes just before serving. *(Serves 6-8)*

 One need not neither sow nor reap fools—they grow freely.

Zucchini Blini

Russian recipe contributed by Regina Kozakova, New York, New York

"I was born in the Soviet Union, in Moscow, in 1940. The main influence in my cooking was my grandfather, Aziz Maksutoff, who lived in Paris to learn the art of belle cuisine. When he returned to Russia, he bought the dining cars on the South-West railroad, linking Russia to Southern Europe. He received a medal from the Queen of Romania for organizing meals for her and her children on their trip across Russia to St. Petersburg.

2 medium-size zucchini
2 eggs
1/4 cup lowfat yogurt
6 Tbsp. all-purpose flour
1 Tbsp. vegetable oil
salt, to taste

freshly ground pepper
(or any black pepper), to taste
5 twigs of parsley, chopped
2 scallions, chopped
1/3 tsp. baking soda, mixed
with a drop of vinegar

(Continued)

(Zucchini Blini continued)

Grate zucchini on a hand grater; put aside. Beat the eggs. Add yogurt and flour. If the batter is not thick enough (consistency of sour cream), add another tablespoon of flour. Mix well. Add grated zucchini, oil, salt, pepper, chopped parsley and scallions. Add the baking soda mixed with a touch of vinegar, right after the batter begins to bubble. Using either a piece of raw potato or onion on a fork, brush a griddle or a frying pan (preferably non-stick) with oil. Make small pancakes; drop from dessert spoon. Flip them on the other side when they are golden brown. They are very good served with the smoked salmon and sour cream or simply with sour cream on the side. **Variations:** Instead of zucchini, it is possible to use either yellow squash, green squash, or apples. Different berries also can be used instead of vegetables. *(Serves 6)*

Stuffed Bell Peppers

Russian recipe contributed by Regina Kozakova, New York, New York

6 bell peppers (2 red, 2 yellow,
  2 green), reserve the tops,
  remove seeds and membrane
corn oil
1 bunch of scallions, chopped
7–8 medium-size carrots, grated
1 medium-size celery root, grated
1 medium-size parsnip,
  (parsley root) grated

1/2 lb. mushrooms, washed, sliced
1 small onion, chopped
1 Tbsp. cognac or brandy
fresh or dried thyme and oregano
salt and pepper, for seasoning
6 cloves of garlic, finely chopped
2 large tomatoes, cut into pieces

Prepare the peppers and set aside. Prepare the stuffing in the corn oil. Sauté the

(Continued)

scallions. Add carrots, celery root, and parsnip. Stir to coat in oil. Cover and cook on top of the stove until almost cooked. In another pan, sauté the onion, adding mushrooms. Stir well. Add cognac or brandy, and cook to evaporate. Season with thyme, oregano, salt and pepper. Mix vegetable stuffing with mushrooms. Stuff the peppers, and put aside. Briefly sauté the garlic, adding the tomatoes. Cook covered. In a deep casserole dish place peppers, open-end up. Cover each one with a top, pour tomato and garlic sauce in between the peppers, cover, and bake for 1 hour at 350°. Cool and serve with nice Italian, French or any hearty, homemade bread. *(Serves 6 as an appetizer; 3 as the main course)*

Prague Red Cabbage

Czech appetizer contributed by the Embassy of the Czech Republic, Washington, D.C.

8–10 slices bacon, cut into strips
1 large onion, finely chopped
1 medium-size head
   of red cabbage, chopped

1 medium-size raw potato, grated
1–1 1/2 cups of red wine
sugar, to taste

Fry the bacon. Add the onion and sauté until light brown. Add the cabbage and stew until soft. Stir in the potato, red wine, and sugar. Cook until potato is done and serve. *(Serves 6-8)*

 The more one sleeps the less one lives.

Ajmpren Cucumbers

Pronounced "im-pren," this is a Slovenian recipe by Marie Prisland, Sheboygan, Wisconsin, contributed by the Slovenian Women's Union of America.

"A dish I was crazy about as a child in Slovenia and still am. This may be served as a main meal or side dish. As a child we were sometimes served a bowl of vegetable or milk soup with it."

2 medium-size cucumbers, peeled, and sliced paper-thin
1 Tbsp. salt
4 medium-size potatoes
2 cups water
1 tsp. salt
2 Tbsp. lard

2 Tbsp. flour
1 1/2 cups potato broth, cracklings (*ocvrki*), if desired
1 tsp. vinegar
1/4 tsp. pepper
1/4 lb. bacon, fried until crisp, crumbled

(Continued)

Peel cucumbers and slice paper-thin into a bowl. Mix in the tablespoon of salt and set aside for at least an hour. Peel the potatoes and cook in 2 cups water and 1 teaspoon salt. When tender, drain, reserve potato broth, and mash.

ROUX:

In a heavy skillet heat the lard. Add flour, stirring constantly, and cook over low heat until golden brown. Gradually stir in the potato broth. (If cracklings are desired, add now.) Add the cucumbers that have been thoroughly squeezed to remove all liquid. Stir in the vinegar and cook for 7 minutes. Stir the mashed potatoes into the mixture until well-blended. Place in serving dish and sprinkle with pepper. Garnish with crumbled bacon. *(Serves 4-6)*

Black Radish Salad

Croatian recipe contributed by Penfield editor, Dorothy Papich Crum, Iowa City, Iowa

These long, black roots are not easy to find on produce shelves, but if one has a small plot, the flavor is worth a short row.

6 large black radishes
salt (preferably Kosher)

olive oil (or other vegetable oil if preferred)

Pare and slice the radishes very thin. Place in a bowl and salt generously. Allow to sit for about 30 minutes, then rinse. Drain as dry as possible. Sprinkle with the oil, toss and serve. *(Serves 4)*

 *Truth is slow but far-reaching.*

Serbian Salad

Serbian recipe from The Congressional Club Cookbook, ©*1927*

A summer dish that can be served as an appetizer or salad with a warm or cold roast.

1 large eggplant (or 2 small)
6 green peppers
1/4 cup olive oil

2 Tbsp. vinegar
salt and black pepper, to taste

Bake eggplant and peppers in the oven as you would bake potatoes (about 45 minutes). Next, remove the outer skin from both, also the seeds from the peppers. Chop the eggplant and peppers. Add olive oil and vinegar. Season with salt and pepper. Mix all well and chill until ready to use. *(Serves 8-10)*

Poultry & Eggs

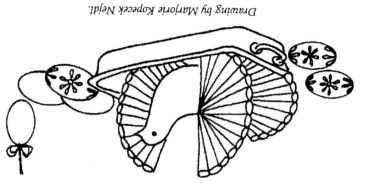

Drawing by Marjorie Kopecek Nejdl.

Chicken Thighs Aziz

Russian recipe contributed by Regina Kozakova, New York, New York

Aziz in Turkish languages means "tender," but this was also the name of my grandfather who was a fine chef and who introduced me to many cuisines. The chicken with the sauce looks very pretty, and it is extremely tasty and light. It is a very good summer entrée with fruit.

12 chicken thighs
4 Tbsp. corn oil (vegetable oil), divided
2 Tbsp. of Scotch or other whiskey
salt, and freshly grated black pepper
fresh, dried thyme

dried rosemary
2 Granny Smith apples, quartered
6 apricots, halved
6 red plums, halved
1 tsp. sugar
1 medium-size white onion, cut into rings

(Continued)

In a dry, hot frying pan, brown chicken thighs. (I prefer chicken thighs because they are juicier.) Brown them well. Pour Scotch or whiskey over the chicken and let evaporate quickly by raising the heat. Season with salt and freshly grated black pepper. Sprinkle with thyme and rosemary. Put aside, loosely covered. Sauté the apples, apricots, and red plums in 2 tablespoons of corn oil. Add sugar. In a roasting pan, sauté the onion in 2 tablespoons corn oil, and add chicken thighs. Pour the fruit sauce over all, and bake for 20 minutes at 325°. Sprinkle with fresh thyme and serve with your choice of a side dish. *(Serves 6)*

Note: Chicken breasts could also be used. Serve with rice or mashed potatoes, carrots, peas, and corn.

Roast Duck

Czech recipe contributed by the Embassy of the Czech Republic, Washington, D.C.

1 duck
salt, seasoning
1 cup water

melted butter, for basting
1–2 Tbsp. flour

Rub the inside of the duck with salt, place in an open pan, and add the water. Bake for approximately 2 hours at 370° to 400°. Baste frequently with the butter and pan juices until the bird is golden brown. Remove the duck. Add flour to pan juices, and cook until thickened.

Tip: Roasting time will depend on the weight. Usually 1/2 hour per pound.

Omelet in Wine

Slovenian recipe by Millie Paisoli, Chicago, Illinois, contributed by the Slovenian Women's Union of America.

This omelet always was prepared for new mothers to give them nourishment. It was a real delicacy in peasant homes. I remember it fondly as being given only on special occasions. We kids rarely got this to eat. It makes a delicious light supper.

2 Tbsp. butter
2 eggs
salt and pepper, to taste

1 Tbsp. Parmesan cheese, grated
1/2 cup white wine

Melt butter in a small omelet pan. In a bowl, beat eggs, salt, pepper, and Parmesan cheese until frothy. When butter is hot, quickly pour in the egg

(Continued)

mixture. Brown on one side, turn over, cover, and brown the other side. It will puff up. After second side is done, pour white wine over omelet and cover for another minute. If you use small amount of wine, the omelet will completely absorb the liquid. If you use 1/2 cup, there will be wine to sop up with toast or bread. It can be served with toast, either way. *(1 serving)*

Chicken with Okra

Bosnian

2 frying chickens, about 2 1/2 lbs.
   each, cut into serving pieces
4 Tbsp. butter or margarine
salt and pepper, to taste
2 large onions, peeled and sliced
1/8 tsp. cayenne pepper

2 cups sliced, uncooked okra
1 cup chopped green peppers
1 cup hot chicken broth
3 Tbsp. tomato paste
3 Tbsp. chopped fresh parsley

Wipe chicken pieces dry and brown on both sides in butter in a skillet. Place chicken into a heavy casserole or Dutch oven. Season with salt and pepper. Sauté onions in drippings. Mix in cayenne; pour over chicken. Top with okra and green

(Continued)

peppers. In another pan, combine 1 cup of hot chicken broth and tomato paste. Bring to a boil; pour over chicken and vegetables. Cook very slowly, covered, about 35 minutes, or until chicken is tender. Add a little more broth during cooking, if necessary. Stir in parsley. *(Serves 4-6)*

Meats & Casseroles

Drawing by Marjorie Kopecek Nejdl.

Sauerkraut Casserole

Slovak dish contributed by Caroline Snauko Verhougstraete of Grand Ledge, Michigan.
Caroline is a grandniece of Monsignor Andrej Hlinka.

1 1/2 lbs. ground beef chuck
1 onion, chopped, browned and
   drained
1 pint can sauerkraut, drained

3/4 cup uncooked rice (white)
1 can tomato soup
1 can water
1 small can V-8 juice (optional)

Mix all ingredients together. Bake at 350° for 1 1/2 hours or until the rice is done.

TIP: If the casserole appears to be getting too dry, add a small can of V-8 juice.
(Serves 6)

Pigs-in-Blankets

Croatian dish contributed by Dorothy Papich Crum, Iowa City, Iowa

2 large heads cabbage
2 lbs. ground beef
1/2 lb. ground pork
1 cup uncooked rice
2 large cloves garlic, minced

salt and pepper, to taste
1 30-oz. can mild sauerkraut
2 bay leaves
1 15-oz. can sauerkraut juice
water to cover

Remove and discard the first layer of leaves of cabbage. Place each head, cord side down, in a deep pot of boiling water. Cook just until tender enough to remove leaves, about 8 minutes. Remove from water and score around the core. Carefully remove large outside leaves. Cut remainder of head (smaller leaves) into wedges.

(Continued)

Mix together the ground beef, pork, rice, garlic, salt and pepper. Shape 1/2 cup portions of meat mixture into balls, and wrap each in a cabbage leaf by rolling and folding sides in before the last lap. Layer rolls in a large pot; spread some of the sauerkraut and cabbage wedges between each layer. Add bay leaves, sauerkraut juice and water. Bring to a boil, reduce to moderate heat and cook slowly for about 2 hours. *(Serves 8-10)*

Meat Stew (Bigos)

Polish recipe by Maria Lemnis and Henryk Vitry.
Contributed by the Embassy of the Republic of Poland, Washington, D.C.

1 1/2 lbs. fresh cabbage, thinly sliced

2 lbs. of assorted meats, cooked, reserving the meat juices: (kielbasa, ham, pork roast, roast beef, or roast duck)

4 large sour apples, peeled, finely chopped

1 cup mushrooms, sliced

2 large onions, finely chopped

1 1/2 lbs. sauerkraut, chopped

1/4–1/2 cup butter or lard

20 prunes, stoned, cut into strips, (or 1–2 Tbsp. plum butter)

2 tsp. sugar (optional)

salt and pepper, to taste

1/3–1/2 cup dry red wine or Madeira

roux of flour, lightly browned

1 Tbsp. thick tomato paste

Bigos *is a composition with many variations in accordance with home traditions. Proportions of meats may vary according to taste, as may proportions of sauerkraut and fresh cabbage.*

Scald the fresh cabbage with boiling water before cooking. Cook in an enameled or cast-iron enameled pot; never in an aluminum one. Cook the cabbage over low heat in a small amount of water, or preferably in the stock from the cooked kielbasa. Add apples and mushrooms to the cabbage and heat along with the stock. Next, lightly brown the onions in lard or butter. Add the onions and sauerkraut to the stock. While the stock is simmering, add prunes or plum butter. Season with salt, pepper and sugar. It should be sharp in taste. Dice the cooked meat and

(Continued)

add to cabbage mixture. Finally, add the red wine or Madeira. Cook the mixture over low heat for 40 minutes, stirring often to prevent burning. Remove from heat and refrigerate. On the second day, reheat the bigos. A roux of flour, lightly browned in fat, may be added to make the bigos thicker. For more seasoning, add a tablespoon of thick tomato paste. It is tastiest after the third reheating.

Pork Roast with Caraway

Polish recipe by Maria Lemnis and Henryk Vitry.
Contributed by the Embassy of the Republic of Poland, Washington, D.C.

2 lbs. pork, cut into a cube
  (do not remove the skin)
salt
large pinch of marjoram

heaping tsp. of caraway seeds
3 Tbsp. butter or lard
2 onions, sliced

Cut pork into a cube. Make shallow incisions in the skin with a sharp knife in a checkerboard pattern. Rub the meat with salt, marjoram and caraway seeds 1 hour before roasting. In a cast-iron pan, heat the lard intensely. Add meat and brown on all sides. Place the browned meat with the skin-side down in a roasting

(Continued)

pan. Add the onions and some boiling water (or broth, if available). Cover and roast at 400°, allowing 30 minutes per pound. During roasting, replenish the evaporated liquid frequently. After 30 minutes of roasting, turn the roast so that the skin is on top and continue roasting—basting with its own sauce from time to time. The incisions in the skin will spread out, forming a checkerboard pattern. Cut the ready roast into thin slices and pour the roast sauce with the onion over it.

Tip: *Kopytka* (see P. 69) goes very well with this roast, as well as buckwheat kasha. Stewed sauerkraut may also be served.

"Wisdom is easy to carry on your shoulders, but it is difficult to load."

Hussar Roast

Polish recipe by Maria Lemnis and Henryk Vitry.
Contributed by the Embassy of the Republic of Poland, Washington, D.C.

2 lbs. roasting meat
juice of 1/2 lemon
flour

Farce (stuffing):
3 medium-size onions, finely
   chopped
2–4 Tbsp. butter

Gravy:
1–2 Tbsp. flour
1 onion, thinly sliced

4 Tbsp. butter
boiling water, for simmering

whole wheat bread, grated
salt and pepper, to taste
1 egg yolk

1/2 cup boiling water

113

(Continued)

Lightly pound a neatly cut piece of roasting meat that is compact in form. Rub with lemon juice, then allow to rest in a cool place for an hour. Dust the meat with flour and fry in butter until browned on all sides. Pour some boiling water into the pan and simmer the meat, covered, for 45 minutes, turning it over from time to time, and adding a little boiling water. When the roast is almost tender, place it on a small board. When the roast is somewhat cooled, slice thinly—only partially through the meat. This will form pockets for stuffing.

To prepare the stuffing: Simmer the onions in butter until tender. Do not brown. Add grated wheat bread and season. Add 1 raw egg yolk to the slightly cooled stuffing. Place the stuffing into every other slit of the meat. Press the roast into its previous shape and smooth the surface with slight pressure.

(Continued)

(Hussar Roast continued)

Gravy: To the sauce which has formed during roasting in the pan, add flour and onion. When the onion becomes tender, add 1/2 cup boiling water. Carefully place the stuffed roast back into the pan with the gravy and cover, and bake in 350° oven for 45 minutes.

To serve: Place the roast on a serving dish. Two slices joined by the stuffing make one portion. Serve the pan gravy separately.

Suggestion: Serve mashed potatoes and sweet, stewed cabbage with apples or tomatoes.

 Friendship is like wine, the older it is the better it is.

Beef Slices (Zrazy) with Mushrooms and Cream

Polish recipe contributed by the Embassy of the Republic of Poland, Washington, D.C.

In Poland, this dish is called a man's breakfast.

1 lb. beef sirloin
3 Tbsp. butter
1/4 cup dried mushrooms
2 cups salted water

salt and pepper, to taste
2 lbs. potatoes, thickly sliced
1/2 pint sour cream
1 rounded tsp. wheat flour

Cut the sirloin into small slices, across the grain. Pound lightly, sprinkle with pepper, and fry briefly in butter. Cook the mushrooms in the salted water until tender. Drain and reserve liquid. Slice the mushrooms, leaving the smaller caps

116

(Continued)

whole. Arrange the meat slices in a saucepan, sprinkling them with the mushrooms, and cover with well-salted mushroom broth. Cover the saucepan tightly and simmer over low heat for 20 minutes. Place the potatoes in the saucepan, cover, shake lightly, and cook over low heat. When the potatoes are nearly tender, add sour cream thoroughly mixed with the wheat flour. Cook covered for another 10 minutes over low heat. You may serve this dish in the saucepan in which it has been prepared. *(Serves 4)*

 There are three things that are difficult to keep hidden: a fire, a cold, and love.

Pork Casserole (Djuveč)

Yugoslavian recipe. Ingredients vary from one region to another.

3 medium-size onions, peeled
  and sliced
1/2 cup olive oil
2 lbs. lean boneless pork,
  cut into 1 1/2-inch cubes
salt and pepper, to taste
1 Tbsp. paprika

6 medium-size tomatoes, peeled
  and sliced
1 medium eggplant, sliced
2 zucchini, sliced
3 green peppers, cleaned and sliced
1 cup sliced green beans
1 cup uncooked rice

Sauté onions in oil until tender. Add pork cubes, and brown. Season with salt, pepper, and paprika. Grease a deep baking dish well. Line the bottom of the dish

(Continued)

with the onion. Place a layer of tomatoes over the onions. Continue adding layers of vegetables until all are used up. Season each layer with salt and pepper. Add the uncooked rice on top of the vegetable layers. Arrange the seasoned meat on top of the bed of rice, topping with a layer of tomato slices. Add enough water to cover ingredients. Bake, covered, in a preheated oven at 350° for about 1 1/2 hours, or until ingredients are cooked. Uncover for last 30 minutes of cooking. *(Serves 6-8)*

Tip: 1/2 cup white wine may be used instead of water to cover ingredients.

Drawing by Marjorie Kopecek Nejdl.

Fish & Seafood

Herring Polish-Style

Polish recipe contributed by the Embassy of the Republic of Poland, Washington, D.C.

Milter herring is the male fish that is ready to breed.

Herring:
4 milter herrings
1 onion, sliced very thin
1 pepper, sliced very thin
1 pimiento, sliced very thin

1 lemon (remove rinds or pits,
   and cut into slices)
1/2 pint sweet cream
juice of 3 lemons
1/2 tsp. powdered sugar

Potatoes: *(served with Herring Polish-Style)*
4 baking potatoes, peeled
oil, brushed on lightly

salt, to taste
caraway seeds, for seasoning

(Continued)

Soak the milter herrings in cold water for 24 hours, changing the water several times while soaking. Remove the skin carefully from the herrings. Remove the milt, put through a wire sieve and reserve. Cut off the tail and head, divide into fillets, and remove the bones. Layer the fillets in a glass dish. Between each layer, place very thin slices of onion, pepper, pimiento, and a slice of lemon. Combine the sweet cream with the juice of 3 large lemons and the herring milt. Do not salt the sauce. Add the powdered sugar. Pour the sauce over the fillets in the dish. Agitate the dish slightly to spread the sauce evenly and cover securely. Place the covered dish in a cool place. After 24 hours, the herrings mature.

Baked potatoes: Peel the potatoes, cover lightly with oil, dust with salt and caraway seed, and bake in a 350° oven for 40–60 minutes.

Salmon Pie

Russian recipe from Regina Kozakova, New York, New York

Stuffing:

1 bunch scallions, chopped, divided
1 bunch parsley, divided
1 bunch dill, divided
2 lbs. fresh salmon
salt, pepper, caraway seeds, and
  peppercorns for seasoning
2 bay leaves, crushed
2 cans beer (your choice)
1/4 cup corn oil
1/4 cup of rice

curry powder, nutmeg, ginger, salt,
  and pepper, for seasoning
  (Additional seasoning optional:
  sesame seeds and coriander)
1/2 cup cold water
1/2 lb. mushrooms, sliced
3 eggs, hard-cooked, and chopped
2 Tbsp. corn oil
pinch of sugar
2 Tbsp. cold water

(Continued)

Dough:

2 oz. yeast

1/2 cup warm water

1 tsp. sugar

6 Tbsp. butter

2 cups flour

1 Tbsp. sour cream

Filling: Make a bed of the chopped scallions, parsley, and dill. Place pieces of salmon on top. Sprinkle them with salt, pepper, caraway seeds, peppercorns and bay leaves. Pour beer over the salmon and poach it in the oven at 400°, about 30 minutes, basting from time to time. Salmon should be cooked well, but not overdone. Sauté rice in corn oil, add curry, nutmeg, ginger, salt and pepper, and cover with 1/2 cup cold water. Cook covered on top of the stove until rice absorbs

(Continued)

the water and is done (about 20 minutes). Remove salmon from roasting pan. Sauté mushrooms lightly in corn oil. Season with salt and pepper. Separate salmon from the bones, remove skin, divide into chunks with your hands. Gently mix together the salmon chunks, cooked rice, cooked mushrooms, and chopped eggs. Add the scallions, dill and parsley to the mixture. Add 2 tablespoons of corn oil, a pinch of sugar, and 2 tablespoons of cold water.

Dough: Dissolve the yeast in lukewarm water with sugar. Let it rise. Mix butter, flour, sour cream, and the yeast liquid. Work well with your hands until it forms a soft ball. Roll immediately to shape into a rectangle (similar to apple strudel). Put the filling lengthwise, pinch in the middle of the pie. To cut designs into the

(Continued)

crust, use a knife or small cookie cutters. Brush it with egg-wash. Preheat the oven to 400°. Bake until it is golden brown. Serve pie with freshly grated horseradish root mixed with either yogurt or mayonnaise on the side. Serve hot. *(Serves 6-8)*

*To believe with certainty,
we must begin with doubting.*

Salmon in Wine with Hollandaise Sauce

Czech recipe contributed by the Embassy of the Czech Republic, Washington, D.C.

2 lbs. of salmon, cut into fillets
white wine, for cooking
allspice, to season
Hollandaise sauce: *(Serves 4)*
5–6 egg yolks
1 stick of butter

peppercorns, to season
1 bay leaf

pinch of white pepper, ground
1 Tbsp. lemon juice

Place salmon in shallow baking dish. Add enough wine to cover. Add seasonings and bake at 400° for approximately 30 minutes.

Sauce: Beat the egg yolks and 1/3 of the butter while cooking in a double boiler. Cook, stirring rapidly, over boiling water till butter melts. Add 1/3 more butter,

(Continued)

stirring constantly. As butter melts, add the remaining butter. When the butter is completely melted, remove pan from water, stirring rapidly for 2 more minutes. Stir in lemon juice. Then stir in white pepper. Heat again over boiling water, stirring constantly for 2–3 minutes.

Tip: If sauce curdles, beat in 1 to 2 tablespoons boiling water.

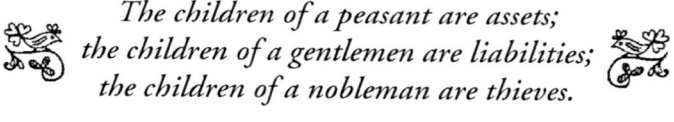

The children of a peasant are assets;
the children of a gentlemen are liabilities;
the children of a nobleman are thieves.

Fish Cutlets with Mushroom Sauce

Russian recipe from The Congressional Club Cookbook, ©1927

3 1/4–4 lbs. freshwater fish,
  deboned, minced fine
1/2 lb. bread, soaked in water
  for 10 minutes

salt and pepper, to taste
2 Tbsp. thick cream
1 egg
breadcrumbs

Mushroom Sauce:
4–6 dried mushrooms
2 whole onions
water, enough to cover
2 Tbsp. butter
1/2 cup flour

1/2 cup sour cream
salt, to taste
fresh mushrooms, finely chopped
  for garnish

(Continued)

Remove crusts from the bread. Soak the remaining bread (soft part) in cold water for about 10 minutes. Mix together the soaked bread, the minced fish, the seasoning, the thick cream, and pass all through a mincer. Then, break 1 egg into the center of this mixture, and mix well together. Shape cutlets about 1 finger-thick in an oblong shape about 4 inches long. Roll cutlets in breadcrumbs and fry in butter in a frying pan, until light brown.

Mushroom Sauce: Place mushrooms into a saucepan with the onions and water, and boil for 1 hour. Then, pass the mushroom bouillon through a sieve. In the meantime, melt 2 tablespoons of butter in a frying pan, add the flour and fry until browned—stirring constantly. Add to this the mushroom bouillon and the sour

(Continued)

(Fish Cutlets with Mushroom Sauce continued)

cream. Boil the whole mixture well, and pass through a colander. Add salt to taste. Garnish with the finely chopped mushrooms.

When serving the fish cutlets: Pour the sauce over the fish cutlets on serving dish.

(Serves 6)

Curried Shrimp

Slovenian recipe of Mary (Marsich) Grilc, Pompano Beach, Florida, contributed by the American Mutual Life Association.

1/4 cup butter, melted
1/4 cup flour
1/2 tsp. salt
dash of paprika
1/2–1 tsp. curry powder
1 1/2 cups milk

3 Tbsp. catsup
1/4 cup sherry wine
1 1/2 cups cleaned, cooked shrimp
   or flaked crab (3/4 lb.)
parsley flakes, for garnish

Blend the butter, flour and seasoning. Gradually stir in the milk. Cook until thick and smooth, stirring constantly. Add the catsup, wine, and shrimp and heat thoroughly. Serve over rice and garnish with parsley flakes. *(Serves 4)*

Baked White Fish with Yogurt Sauce

Yugoslavian

1 4-lb. whole white fish, cleaned
  and skinned
3 onions, peeled and sliced
3 cloves garlic, minced
1/3 cup olive oil
1 Tbsp. paprika
3 Tbsp. tomato paste

3 Tbsp. fresh parsley, chopped
salt and pepper, to taste
1 cup dry white wine or water
2 Tbsp. flour
1 cup yogurt

Place fish in a greased baking dish. In a frying pan, sauté onions and garlic in hot oil until tender. Add paprika; cook 1 minute. Stir in tomato paste, parsley, salt, pepper, and wine. Pour over fish. Bake in a preheated 350° oven, allowing about 10 minutes per pound, until tender, basting occasionally with pan juices. Remove fish to a hot platter. Stir flour into pan juices. Add yogurt; mix well. Cook over low heat, stirring, for 5 minutes. Pour a small amount of sauce over fish. Serve remaining sauce on the side. *(Serves 4)*

Desserts & Pastries

Drawing by Marjorie Kopecek Nejdl.

Two-Hour Nut Rolls (Kolacki)

Slovak treat contributed by Caroline Sauko Verhougstraete of Grand Ledge, Michigan.

2 cakes yeast
1/2 cup warm milk
6 cups flour, sifted
1 cup butter or margarine
1 tsp. salt
3 Tbsp. sugar

3 eggs, beaten
1 cup sour cream or canned milk
nut filling (See pp. 43 or 153) or
   prepared canned poppyseed
   filling
powdered sugar (optional)

Dissolve yeast in milk. Combine flour, butter, salt, sugar, eggs, and sour cream. Add the yeast and milk mixture. Blend well by kneading for approximately 10 minutes. Divide dough into 4 parts and roll out each part approximately 1/4 inch

(Continued)

(Two-Hour Nut Rolls continued)

thick. Spread with nut or poppyseed mixture. Roll and place seam-side down on greased pan and allow to rise 1 hour or until about double. Bake 35–40 minutes at 350°. Sprinkle with powdered sugar after it has cooled and before serving. Slice.

TIP: This can be frozen. To thaw: wrap in foil and heat at 400° for about 5 minutes.

 You can travel far with a lie, but if discovered, how will you travel back?

Slovak Slices

Slovak recipe contributed by Dorothy Jurcenko of Chicago, Illinois

2 cups butter
2 cups granulated sugar
4 egg yolks
4 cups all-purpose flour

2 cups chopped walnuts
2 cans (14 oz.) fruit pastry filling
powdered sugar

Preheat oven to 350°. Cream butter and sugar in large bowl until fluffy. Add egg yolks and mix well with wooden spoon. Add flour and nuts. Grease a 9x13-inch pan. Spread half the dough in the bottom of the pan. Add a layer of pastry filling. Add other half of the dough over the filling. Bake 35–40 minutes, until nicely browned. Cool. Cut into squares. Sprinkle with powdered sugar. *(Makes 36 squares)*

Raised Doughnuts (Krofe)

Slovenian treat contributed by Alice Kuhar, Cleveland, Ohio

Krofe is my mother's recipe which she brought with her from Slovenia in 1929 and perfected through the years. She was well-known for her delicious krofe and was asked many times to prepare them for friends' weddings, parties, and anniversaries.

1 large cake compressed yeast
5 Tbsp. sugar, divided
6 Tbsp. sweet butter
2 cups milk
6 egg yolks
1/2 pint sour cream

6 cups sifted, all-purpose flour
2 tsp. salt
Crisco for frying
powdered sugar, sifted
  (for topping)

(Continued)

Crumble yeast in a bowl with 2 tablespoons of sugar. In a saucepan heat butter and milk, only until butter melts. Cool slightly, then pour about 1 1/2 cups of this mixture over the yeast and stir until yeast is dissolved. Set aside until frothy. Set aside the pan with remaining milk. Mix together thoroughly, the egg yolks and sour cream. Sift together flour, remaining sugar, and salt. Place about 4 cups of this mixture in a large mixing bowl. Set remaining 2 cups aside to add while beating. Next, make a well in the bowl of flour. Mixing with a wooden spoon, add the milk-butter mixture from the saucepan; stir in yeast mixture and continue mixing until all dry ingredients are moistened. Beat with wooden spoon (air bubbles will make crackling sounds). Slowly add reserved flour and continue to beat well after each addition. Keep beating until wooden spoon will stand

(Continued)

alone in the batter and the dough begins to tear off the spoon. (Beating will take about 20 minutes.) Cover and let rise in a warm place until doubled, at least 2 hours or more if possible. Cover half of your table with a clean white cloth. On the other half, lightly flour a large bread board, or use another clean cloth. When dough has risen, flour your hands and place dough onto the board or cloth. Do not roll the dough. Start pulling out a portion from the edge of the dough gently, a little at a time, patting until it's about 1/2 to 3/4 inch thick. Using the edge of a glass or doughnut cutter, cut out *krofe*, flouring the edge of the cutter each time. Pat rounds of dough into shape and place on clean cloth; cover with another cloth. Continue to pull edges of dough and cutting. Keep shaped doughnuts covered and when done, let them rest awhile—about 30 minutes. Fry remaining

(Continued)

dough ends as they are, or pat them together to make additional rounds. Place paper towels on a flat surface for draining, after frying. Place Crisco (about 1 to 2 lbs.) in a deep frying container, or place in an electric skillet and heat. To test temperature, fry the ends to see if they brown nicely. Now fry your doughnuts, starting with the first ones that were cut. When the bottom is a golden brown, flip lightly with slotted spoon and fry top side. When fried, remove and place on paper towels. Sprinkle with sifted powdered sugar when ready to serve.

To reheat frozen *krofe*: Place frozen *krofe* on cookie sheet in preheated 375° oven for 10–12 minutes until warmed through.

For a few days-old *krofe*: Heat oven to 350° and heat for 10 minutes.

Kolaches

Czech recipe contributed by Ed Nejdl of Cedar Rapids, Iowa

A Smithsonian representative visited Marj Nejdl decorating eggs and found Ed, her husband, making kolaches in the kitchen. The representative told Marj that alongside her egg decoration, it would be nice to have Ed demonstrate the art of making kolaches at the Smithsonian Folk Life Festival 1996, in Washington D.C., which included a group from Iowa celebrating the Iowa Sesquicentennial.

2 cups milk (scalded)
2/3 cup sugar
2 pkgs. dry yeast
1 1/2 tsps. salt
1 whole egg

2 egg yolks
1/3 cup butter
1/3 cup chicken fat (or butter)
6 cups flour, divided
melted butter

143

(Continued)

(Kolaches continued)

Scald milk, and add sugar. When cooled to lukewarm, add yeast and let rise. Add the other ingredients; divide flour by half and add the last half of the flour after the rest has been mixed evenly. Use bread hook mixer or wooden spoon. Store in refrigerator overnight. Then, make dough into small balls—the size of walnuts. Grease the balls. Place on greased cookie sheet and let rise until doubled in size. Then, press the center of ball, making an indentation, leaving rim on outer circle. Fill with filling of your choice. Let rise again until light. Bake at 425° for 12 minutes. Brush top with melted butter. *(Makes about 5 dozen)*

"A father's blessing cannot be drowned by water nor consumed by fire."

Fruit Cobbler

Slavic dessert recipe contributed by Helen Timo, Bentleyville, Pennsylvania

Fruit:
3 cups peaches or apples,
   peeled, sliced
3/4 cup sugar

1/2–3/4 stick butter
   (or margarine), softened

Pastry:
2/3 cup sugar
1/2 cup flour, not sifted
2 tsp. baking powder

pinch of salt
3/4 cup milk

(Continued)

(Fruit Cobbler continued)

Mix fruit, 3/4 cup sugar, and butter; let stand. **Pastry:** Mix 2/3 cup sugar, flour, baking powder, salt, and milk and pour into an ungreased 8x8-inch baking dish. Cover with the fruit mixture and bake at 350° for 1 hour. Turn out to cool.

Honey Cake (Medovnik)

Ukrainian dessert contributed by Helen Timo, Bentleyville, Pennsylvania

1 cup butter
1 cup white or brown sugar
6 eggs, separated
1 cup honey
1 cup sour cream
3 1/4 cups sifted flour
2 tsp. baking powder

2 tsp. baking soda
1 tsp. nutmeg
1 tsp. cinnamon
1/4 tsp. salt
1 cup walnuts, chopped
1 tsp. vanilla

Cream butter and sugar. Add egg yolks, one at a time, beating well after each addition. Stir in honey and sour cream. Sift flour with baking powder, baking

147

(Continued)

soda, nutmeg, cinnamon, and salt. Mix 1 tablespoon of flour mixture with nuts. Add sifted dry ingredients to egg mixture. Mix well. Add walnuts, and vanilla. Beat egg whites until stiff and fold into batter. Spoon batter into a greased 10-inch tube pan. Bake at 350° for 1 hour.

Bow Pastry (Cheregi)

Slavic treat contributed by Helen Timo, Bentleyville, Pennsylvania

1/4 lb. butter, softened
1 cup sugar
3 eggs
1/2 pint sour cream
1 tsp. vanilla

4 to 4 1/2 cups flour
3 heaping tsp. baking powder
1/2 tsp. salt
fat, for deep fat frying
powdered sugar

Mix all ingredients, except fat and powdered sugar. Using 4 to 4 1/2 cups of flour, knead mixture to dough consistency. Roll out dough about 1/8 inch thick. Cut dough into small squares. Make a cut with a knife in the center and draw one of the corners through to make a bow. Fry in deep fat until golden brown. Drain. Dust with powdered sugar.

Apricot Dumplings

Czech dessert contributed by the Embassy of the Czech Republic, Washington, D.C.

2 8-oz. pkgs. Philadelphia cream
    cheese
2 cups flour (preferably Wondra)
1 egg

18–20 apricots, pitted
pinch of salt
sour cream mixed with sugar,
    to taste

Combine the Philadelphia cream cheese, flour, and egg into dough, and form into a roll. This will be the dough for your dumplings. Pinch off pieces and flatten these into circles about 2 inches in diameter. Wrap each around an apricot, encasing it securely. Bring a large pot of water to boil, and add a pinch of salt.

(Continued)

Then, add the dumplings. They will sink and eventually surface. From that point, boil them 5–7 more minutes, then remove them with a perforated spoon. Drain and serve with sour cream mixed with sugar.

Nut Butterhorns (Kifli)

Slovenian recipe of Anne Kompare, Chicago, Illinois, contributed by the Slovenian Women's Union of America.

2 cups sifted all-purpose flour
1/4 tsp. salt
1 cake (5/8 oz.) compressed
  yeast

1/2 cup butter
2 egg yolks
1/2 cup sour cream

Filling:

1 cup walnuts, finely ground
1/2 cup sugar

2 egg whites, stiffly beaten
1 tsp. vanilla

Sift flour and salt into mixing bowl. Crumble in yeast. Cut in butter with a pastry

(Continued)

blender until mixture is crumbly. Add egg yolks and sour cream and mix well. Form into a ball. Place on a lightly floured board or pastry cloth. Knead until smooth, about 5 minutes. Divide dough into 3 parts. Wrap in waxed paper and chill for two hours or so. Heat oven to 375°.

Filling: Combine walnuts and sugar. Fold into stiffly beaten egg whites. Add vanilla and blend. Set aside. Sprinkle pastry canvas with powdered sugar and roll each part of dough into a 9-inch circle; cut each into 8 pie-shaped wedges. Fill the wide end of each wedge with a rounded teaspoon of filling and roll from wide end to the point. Tuck point underneath. Place on lightly greased baking sheet and brush with melted butter. Bake in 375° oven for 20 to 25 minutes or until golden brown. Dust with powdered sugar. *(Makes 24)*

Pupaky (Bubalky)

From the menu of a Slovak supper contributed by Cecilia Gaughan, Whitehall, Pennsylvania, of the Ladies Pennsylvania Slovak Catholic Union.

2 cakes compressed yeast,
   broken into pieces
1 tsp. sugar
1/4 cup warm water
1 pint of milk, or 1 can condensed
   milk plus 1 cup water
1 Tbsp. salt
3 cups flour
3 large eggs, separated

1 cup sugar
1/2 lb. shortening
   (butter, margarine, Crisco)
4–5 cups flour
ground nuts or poppyseed and
   sugar mixture
boiling milk for dipping
honey, topping

154

(Continued)

Mix yeast, sugar, and 1/4 cup warm water. Cover and let stand to rise. Meanwhile, warm the milk. Add salt and flour; beat with wooden spoon, add the raised yeast, and mix well for at least 5 minutes. Cover and let stand in a warm place while you prepare the following: Beat the egg yolks well. Then add sugar and beat again. Separately, beat the egg whites until they form peaks. Melt the shortening and when cooled, add to the raised dough. Mix well and add the egg and sugar mixture. Then fold in the egg whites. Add flour till thickened and keep mixing for about 15 minutes until the dough does not stick to the spoon or your hands. Add more flour as needed. Cover and let stand for at least 2 hours. (3 or 3 1/2 hours won't hurt.)

(Continued)

(Pupaky continued)

To make *Pupaky:* Flatten pieces of dough with your hands. Cut into 1" strips and roll between your hands to form balls. Drop close together onto greased baking pans and let rise about 1 hour. Bake at 350° about 20 minutes or until nice and light brown. When cool, pull apart and drop into boiling milk a few at a time to absorb milk. Remove with sieve and sprinkle ground nuts and sugar mixture over *pupaky;* or ground poppyseed and sugar mixture. Spoon honey on top when ready to eat. (*Great recipe to serve at a large holiday gathering.*)

 A mighty river owes its power to the little brooks.

Putrovničky (Kiffels)

Slovak recipe contributed by the Ladies Pennsylvania Slovak Catholic Union

3 tsp. sugar, divided
1 cake compressed yeast
1/2 cup lukewarm water
4 cups flour
1 tsp. salt

1 lb. shortening (combine half
  butter, margarine, or lard)
4 egg yolks (save whites for nuts)
1/2 pint sour cream
1 tsp. vanilla
nut filling (recipes pp. 43 & 153)

Put 1/2 teaspoon sugar in cup or small bowl, and break yeast into it. Add 1/2 cup warm water; cover and let stand until it rises. Sift flour; add salt and remaining sugar. Cut shortening into flour (same as for pies). When consistency is like

(Continued)

cracker meal, make a well and put in egg yolks, sour cream, vanilla, and yeast mixture. Mix all ingredients (hands work best), working the dough until it doesn't stick to surface. You may add some flour. Cut dough into 4 or 6 pieces, about 5"x6" in size. Put in refrigerator or freezer overnight, but take out of freezer to defrost, at least 5 hours before rolling. Roll out 1 piece at a time to desired thickness. Cut into 2 1/2 x 3 1/2-inch pieces; fill with nut filling and roll up. Put on lightly greased baking pans. Bake at 350° for 15 minutes. They are done when nicely browned. Adjust time up to 15 minutes more, or as your oven needs.

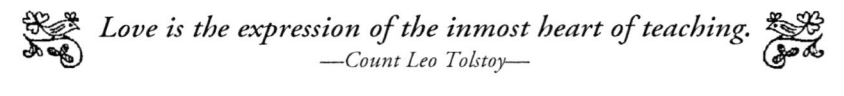

Love is the expression of the inmost heart of teaching.
—*Count Leo Tolstoy*—